It is with great joy that I rec
latest book, Faith for Assignme
tiny with Courage and Clarity. *Having known Vidar since his graduation from Rhema Bible Training College in 2002, I have witnessed firsthand his unwavering commitment to spreading the Gospel and empowering believers worldwide.*

Faith for Assignments *is not just another book on faith; it is a profound exploration of Hebrews 11, inviting readers to walk in the footsteps of the heroes of old while embracing the unique assignments and callings placed upon each of our lives. Drawing from his extensive experience in establishing Rhema Bible Training College campuses throughout East Africa, Vidar challenges us to believe God not only for salvation, healing, and provision but also for the courage to step out in faith and fulfill our divine assignments.*

In a world filled with uncertainty and doubt, Faith for Assignments *will strengthen your faith in the promises of God. As you begin this transformational journey through the pages of this book, be inspired to embrace your calling with courage, clarity, and unwavering faith.*

I wholeheartedly encourage you to read Faith for Assignments *and allow its powerful message to ignite a renewed sense of purpose and passion within your heart.*

—Kenneth W. Hagin
Pastor, Rhema Bible Church and President Rhema Bible Training College

One day, we will stand before God's judgment seat and give an account of our lives and ministries. This book is one of the precious witnesses our Father God has prepared to help us get ready for that encounter. In it, we learn that faith isn't just something we use to get things but to fulfill the plans and purposes of God for our lives and be a blessing to others. I highly recommend it.

—Tokunbo Adejuwon, Director Rhema Nigeria

I have known Vidar for over 20 years. There are a few people that I know who truly inspire me and Vidar is one of those. I have been amazed to watch and see firsthand what faith in God has allowed Vidar and Cathrine to accomplish in East Africa.

There has always been something in me that was never satisfied with status quo. I don't want to be normal; I want to go forward and accomplish things that have never been done before. Too many of us sit back and celebrate the heroes of the past instead of allowing them to inspire us for greater. Certainly, we are to honor them for the trails that they blazed, but the greatest honor we can bestow on them is to pick up where they left off and go even further. I don't know about you, but I want to be one to inspire my generation and future generations to go further. God wants to see your name in the Hall of Faith too!

I highly recommend Faith For Assignments. *God has an assignment for you and He needs you to fulfill it. In this powerful book, Vidar gives you scriptural and yet practical keys to overcome normal, fulfill all God has called you to, and advance into a life of greater works.*

—Chad Gonzales, D.Min, President of Chad Gonzales Ministries and Founder of The Healing Academy

In this book, Faith For Assignments, *Vidar Ligard shares his story of his journey of faith as he pursued his divine assignment. His courage pushed him to overcome challenges, take risks, and pioneer the birth of many Bible schools that have impacted many lives.*

I recommend this book to anyone who desires to step out and launch into the deep, start new businesses, shift ministry to another level, and change their life. Get ready for a transformative shift in your thinking and faith.

—Bishop Thomas B. Imende
New Hope Outreach Ministries, Nairobi, Kenya

Rev. Vidar calls us to join the heroes of faith from the past, to step out of our comfort zones and believe in God's power to do the extraordinary. He embodies the message he preaches, and if Hebrews 11 were written today, I'm certain Vidar and Cathrine would be mentioned alongside those historic figures of faith.

My challenge to you is not only to read this book but to internalize its message, accept its challenges, step out in faith, and dare to believe that God will fulfill His promises in you as you push past ordinary limits and overcome any obstacle in your path.

—David Fowler
Pastor of Remnant Church, Manhattan, KS

This is not an ordinary book. Faith For Assignments *will build your faith and give you the passion to step out into your God-given assignment. It will give you the knowledge you need and build your faith in order to achieve your purpose in life. This book is a must-read and a great tool for people who seriously want to make a difference in life as they fulfill their divine assignment.*

—William Meni
Bishop of Jesus Warriors Church,
Mombasa Kenya and Missionary to the DRC

There are very few people like Reverend Vidar who embody the virtues of excellence, growth and continuous improvement—people who will constantly encourage you to push past your comfort, and rise to the next level. Vidar's wisdom and insight have been a guiding light in my own personal and ministerial growth.

In this inspiring book, Vidar provides fresh insight on the life of faith, how to grow exceedingly in our faith and confidence in God, and how to never settle, stop, or become comfortable with just enough. Push past mediocrity and strive for God's very best in our lives.

I encourage you to allow yourself to be stretched by taking careful consideration of the tools presented through these wonderful pages. As you read this book, I believe you will find new passion and determination to fulfill your assignment.

—David Crammer
Senior Pastor Covenant Life Church, Chandler, AZ

FAITH FOR ASSIGNMENTS

Embracing Your Divine Journey with Courage and Clarity

VIDAR LIGARD

Tulsa, OK, USA

Faith for Assignments: Embracing Your Divine Journey With Courage And Clarity

ISBN: 978-1-7348655-4-7 (Paperback printed in the USA)

Published by Safari Mission.
Tulsa, OK, USA.
www.safarimission.org

Library of Congress Control Number: 2024934895

To all those who refuse to be bound by limits

CONTENTS

PREFACE

There is more to faith than just believing God exists, and there is more to the Christian life than just living an overall healthy and good life, providing for our families. There is actually *a lot* more!

When God called us, He not only gave us Christ as a sacrifice for our sins, but with Him, He gave us all things that pertain to life and godliness. Then He called us to go into all the world and proclaim the good news of what Christ has done for humanity. We should be living in such a way that we leave a remarkable impact on those around us.

Over the years, I have observed so many believers who start out well, but all too often get stuck somewhere along the way, settle down, and accept less than what God has for them. Not only have I seen the frustration that goes along with settling down, but there are also the ramifications of lost opportunities and all the lives that could have and should have been impacted for the better.

Through these pages, it is my desire that you find a new passion and desire to go further than you ever thought possible.

The lives of others depend on *YOU*!

God bless you!

Vidar Ligard

And this is the victory that has overcome the world —our faith.

CHAPTER ONE

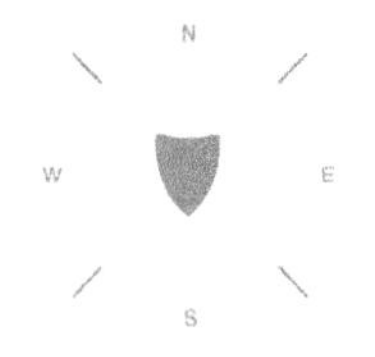

Levels of Faith

Now faith is the assurance of things hoped for, the conviction of things not seen.

Hebrews 11:1

And without faith it is impossible to please him, for whoever would draw near to God must believe that he exists and that he rewards those who seek him.

Hebrews 11:6

Real faith—Bible faith—is an unwavering confidence that what God said in His Word is the truth. Those who truly believe are so sure of this conviction that they know it to be true even if their physical senses cannot prove it.

It's a conviction that is so strong it causes us to speak. It causes us to act in line with what we have in our heart. Real faith is of the heart—a conviction not based on science or natural evidence, but based on evidence of what God has said. Real faith isn't, "I think so" or "I hope so." It's a conviction so strong that it enables us to walk out what God has said, regardless of what other voices in this world are telling us, regardless of what friends are telling us, or regardless of what science is telling us.

I will qualify this by saying I believe in science. I studied science. I earned my bachelor of science degree in engineering from Oral Roberts University. I have done rocket research for NASA. I have designed advanced microprocessors and math coprocessors. I've even been part of teams designing advanced guided missile systems. So, yes, I do believe in science, but there is a voice that is far more important—a voice mightier and weightier than any other voice. And when we believe that voice over all others, we call that faith, resting assured that what God has told us is true.

God told us this kind of faith pleases Him. Hebrews 11:6 tells us, "And without faith it is impossible to please him, for whoever would draw near to God must believe that he exists and that he rewards those who seek him."

Living by faith is critical to life. The Bible explains that we are saved by faith,[1] we walk by faith,[2] we live by faith,[3]

1 Eph. 2:8
2 2 Cor. 5:7
3 Rom. 1:17

we obtain promises by faith,[4] and we conquer mountains by faith.[5] Faith makes the impossible possible. Nothing is impossible for those who believe.[6] Jesus spoke of greater works and miracles that should follow those who believe.[7]

Yet, so many only grasp some of the things God expects us to walk in by faith.

The walk of faith has different levels and different depths. Someone can go swim in a pool. Someone else can venture out to a lake, find some waist deep water, and swim there. Others could go further, head to the ocean and swim away from shore. In essence, all swimming is the same, but there is still a big difference between swimming in a pool and swimming far out from the ocean shore where there are waves and no security of having the ability to rest our feet at the bottom.

One time, I was on a ship, somewhere between Norway and Denmark where we could not see shore anywhere. Some friends and I jumped overboard to go swimming. One of the sailors on board thought he would prank us by pulling the ladder up from the side of the ship. Here we were swimming in the ocean. I could see nothing but sky, water, a couple of my friends' heads bobbing in the water, and this ship I had no way of accessing. This sure brought

4 Heb. 11:33
5 Matt. 17:20
6 Mark 9:23
7 John 14:12

swimming to a whole different level when there seemed to be no security anywhere around. There was an awe in the magnitude of the sky and the ocean, and in the middle of it all, I felt so small. Fear wanted to grip me with the thought *Your life now totally depends on your friend eventually bringing the ladder back down.*

The principles of swimming are the same whether I swim in the comfort of a safe pool or in the vastness of the ocean far from shore, yet there is a *vast* difference in these experiences. Similarly, there are different levels of faith, and God desires that we continually grow in our faith and confidence in Him.

The first level of faith begins when we are saved by faith. It is a marvelous thing to be convinced that what Christ did for me on the cross is sufficient for my sins to be washed away, and my fellowship with God restored so I can enter His throne with confidence. Being born again is moving from being convinced that God simply exists to believing Christ paid for my personal sins, and by accepting Him as savior, I now have a personal relationship with God.

Being innocent is a marvelous state to be in. When there is no sin, it becomes easy to walk and talk with God the way Adam and Eve did in the garden. As a newborn baby, there are no worries and there are no walls to put up in any relationships. This is righteousness—the ability to stand in the presence of God as if sin never existed.

Many try so hard to get closer to God or simply just to please Him, but often feel they are not quite measuring up. Typically, they either settle for a relationship with God that seems distant, or they try feverishly to grow closer. The Apostle Paul flawlessly followed the Mosaic Law. If there was anyone who could be right with God by his own actions, it would be him. Yet, despite all of his achievements, look at what he wrote in Philippians 3.

> **Indeed, I count everything as loss because of the surpassing worth of knowing Christ Jesus my Lord. For his sake I have suffered the loss of all things and count them as rubbish, in order that I may gain Christ and be found in him, not having a righteousness of my own that comes from the law, but that which comes through faith in Christ, the righteousness from God that depends on faith—that I may know him and the power of his resurrection.**
>
> **Philippians 3:8–10**

Real faith starts when we rest in the assurance that our relationship with God is not based on who we are or what we have done, but we trust and know that Christ lived a perfect life, fully innocent, and became our substitute, when He took upon Himself our identity on the cross and paved the way for us to be fully innocent in the presence of God.

The truth of the all-sufficiency of Christ's sacrifice, and that we "become the righteousness of God"[8]—the very core of the Gospel—must be defended in every generation, just like John Owen did in 1677 when he wrote *Doctrine of Justification by Faith*, E.W Kenyon in 1942 when he wrote *Two Kinds of Righteousness*, and John Piper in 2002 with *Counted Righteous in Christ*. Reading after Piper's defense of this truth, Professor Mark Talbot wrote, "Although I have been a Christian for a long time, I became aware of the doctrine of the imputation of Christ's active righteousness only fairly recently. Yet in the years since I have become aware of the 'Blessed Exchange'—my sin for Christ's righteousness—I doubt that a day has gone by without my feasting on this core truth of biblical faith."[9]

Not only does the truth of salvation by faith need to be defended in every generation, it must also be meditated upon and defended in our own minds and lives each and every day. It's difficult to swim in the ocean if we cannot master the swimming pool. Likewise, knowing that our relationship with God is based on what Christ did becomes an anchor that gives daily peace, strength, and courage to go onto the deeper things.

8 2 Cor. 5:21
9 John Piper "Counted Righteous in Christ: Should we abandon the Imputation of Christ's Righteousness" Paperback edition 2002, one of the praise testimonies inside the front cover.

We are saved by faith, but we are not only saved by faith, but we walk by faith[10] and we obtain promises by faith.[11] We call Hebrews 11 the "Hall of Faith" because it is filled with references to the Old Testament people of faith, like Abel, Enoch, Noah, Abraham, Sarah, Moses, David, Rahab, and so on.

Abraham is not only in the Hall of Faith, but he is also known as the Father of Faith because over 50 percent of the world's population—Christians, Jews, and Muslims—all refer to him as father. The Bible tells of how Abraham "*believed God and it was counted to him as righteousness*."[12] But Abraham's faith did not end with faith for righteousness alone.

Abraham had no heir, and it was biologically impossible for him and Sarah to have children. Yet, God gave him the promise, "*Look toward heaven, and number the stars ... So shall your offspring be*."[13] God further promised to give Abraham the land to possess.[14]

All throughout Scripture, we find the promises of God, and He desires for us to trust Him and experience the fulfillment of these promises. God sealed His promise to Abraham with a covenant,[15] showing Abraham that his Word is fully dependable.

10 2 Cor 5:7
11 Heb. 11:33
12 Gen. 15:6, Rom. 4:3, Gal. 3:6
13 Gen. 15:5
14 Gen. 15:7
15 Gen. 15:8–21

Abraham had walked with God since he was 75 years old, but at 85, he still had no son. That is when Sarah and Abraham decided to implement plan B. Plan B is an alternative we tend to have in mind, that if things happen to not work out according to God's Word, our alternative will have to suffice. In business negotiations, we call it the BATNA—the Best Alternative to a Negotiated Agreement. When believing for God's best, too many times we settle for what *looks like* the best, but it's just an inferior version of God's promise. So at 85, Abraham had a child through Hagar, Sarah's servant, and Ishmael was born. Having a child through your wife's servant was a common alternative to infertility in that day and age, but it still wasn't what God promised.

While Abraham had now walked with God for quite a while, God still needed to help him change his mindset so he could receive what God had truly promised. So, at age 99, God changed Abram's name to Abraham. When we say anyone's name today, we often don't think about the meaning, but both Abram and Abraham are Hebrew names where the meaning is evident to anyone who speaks the language. So his name was changed from "Blessed Father" to "Father of a Multitude." But in order for this name change to take effect, Abraham would have to announce and explain to his family, friends, and all of his employees that he was now "Father of a Multitude." No longer could the promise be in his mind as he looked at the stars, but he had to put the promise in his mouth. As God told Abraham of the name change, He also said, "for I have made you the father of a multitude of nations."[16] It is an important detail of language that God already counted it as a fact that Abraham had been made a father before the promised son was even born. Faith is a conviction of the heart that is so strong that you count what you are believing as done even before you can see it. Paul wrote about Abraham in Romans 4, "he grew strong in his faith as he gave glory to God, fully convinced that God was able to do what he had promised."[17] After Abraham changed what he said about himself on a daily basis, Sarah became pregnant just a few months later and soon after, Isaac was born.

The Bible is full of promises and miracles that were not absolutely necessary. Jesus did not *have* to walk on the water. He could have walked around the Sea of Galilee just like all the people did. It wasn't *necessary* to curse the fig tree. Some have thought He did so to create a faith object lesson, but that could not be the reason because John said there were so many miracles that all the books of the world could not contain all the stories.[18] It also was not necessary to feed the 5000, because it was completely within reason to send the people home, just as the disciples proposed. The Old Testament also has God's interventions recorded when they were honestly not necessary. Elisha made the lost

16 Gen. 17:5
17 Rom. 4:20-21
18 John 21:25

ax head float so his protege could retrieve it and keep building a house. Joshua made the sun stand still. Solomon made silver so common that they didn't even bother to count it. God did all of this and much more because He delights in us having promises come to pass in our daily life.

Just consider for a moment these Scriptures, talking about the promises of God:

> **For all the promises of God find their Yes in him. That is why it is through him that we utter our Amen to God for his glory.**
>
> **2 Corinthians 1:20**

> **Since we have these promises, beloved, let us cleanse ourselves from every defilement of body and spirit, bringing holiness to completion in the fear of God.**
>
> **2 Corinthians 7:1**

> **So that you may not be sluggish, but imitators of those who through faith and patience inherit the promises.**
>
> **Hebrews 6:12**

> **By which he has granted to us his precious and very great promises, so that through**

them you may become partakers of the divine nature, having escaped from the corruption that is in the world because of sinful desire.

2 Peter 1:4

Scripture repeatedly talks about the many promises of God, and then it declares:

Let us hold fast the confession of our hope without wavering, for he who promised is faithful.

Hebrews 10:23

Not only did He make many and great promises, but He is faithful and true to bring to pass what He has promised.

So, let us not be like the 10 spies who brought back an evil report,[19] but let us rather be like Joshua and Caleb who believed the promises, spoke in line with God's promises, and possessed those promises. That is the kind of faith that God delights in.

Beyond learning to trust God for our relationship with Him, and beyond learning to trust Him for what He has promised in our lives, there is another level that is not very

19 Num. 13:32 (KJV) calls it "an evil report." Many other translations call it "a bad report." It was a report contrary to God's promise to the nation. Because the spies were neither ignorant of this promise nor of the power and the faithfulness of God, they were not just bringing back a negative report as they saw it, they had refused to believe God, and this is not just bad or negative, it truly is evil or sin. This is explained further in Hebrews 3:7–19 where the writer warns "do not harden your hearts," and to take care "lest there be in any of you an evil, unbelieving heart."

often talked about. I call it faith for assignments. Life is not just about our new leather sofa, a larger home, or a new car. It is not just about obtaining promises for our own personal lives. Those promises are there and we do need to believe in those and for those. We need to act upon those and set those things as examples for others to follow, but there is more. There is faith for the assignments God has given each of us.

After describing the common life concerns of having food, clothing, and the basic necessities of life, Jesus declared in Matthew 6:33, *"But seek first the kingdom of God and his righteousness, and all these things will be added to you."*

In other words, our focus should be on God's kingdom and the expansion of it, and this should take priority over the focus on our own needs. The Hall of Faith in Hebrews 11 spends much more time telling the stories of faith for assignments than it does of faith for personal promises. The stories of Gideon, Barak, Samson, Jephtah, David, Samuel, and all the prophets are stories of how they walked with God and through their faith in Him were able to affect the lives of the people around them.

When Paul wrote to the Ephesians about faith, redemption, grace, and works, he said:

For by grace you have been saved through

faith. And this is not your own doing; it is the gift of God, not a result of works, so that no one may boast. For we are his workmanship, created in Christ Jesus for good works, which God prepared beforehand, that we should walk in them.

Ephesians 2:8–10

In other words, salvation is a result of faith and grace, and it does not come from anything we have done or can do. Yet, once saved, we do not simply passively rejoice that we are saved and not let our salvation produce any change in our lives. A true salvation always leads to a changed life. So, we move beyond the new birth experience and then focus on allowing God's life in us to affect the lives of others around us through how we live. Think about Abraham and Sarah.

Yes, Abraham believed God and it was counted to him as righteousness. Yes, Sarah believed God and she had Isaac when she had been barren. But, Abraham and Sarah also gave us examples on how to leave one culture and people in order to be obedient to God. They also gave us the example of risking everything they had in order to follow Him. Abraham and Sarah had faith for assignments and you can too!

CHAPTER TWO

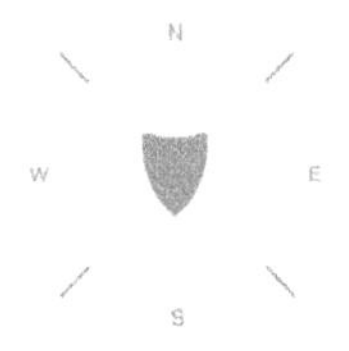

Join the Heroes

We Are Invited into the Hall of Faith

The Hall of Faith, as we call it from Hebrews 11, is not complete. After briefly telling their stories, the writer added, *"God had a better plan for us: that their faith and our faith would come together to make one completed whole, their lives of faith not complete apart from ours."*[20] You and I are needed to make the Hall of Faith complete.

The author continued in the next chapter:

> **Therefore, since we are surrounded by such a great cloud of witnesses, let us also lay aside every weight and sin which clings so closely, and let us run with endurance the race that is set before us.**
>
> **Looking to Jesus, the founder and perfecter of faith, who for the joy that was set before**

20 Heb. 11:40 (MSG)

Him endured the cross, despising the shame, and is seated at the right hand of the throne of God.

Hebrews 12:1–2

You and I are needed to make the Hall of Faith complete.

We are surrounded by the witnesses of Hebrews 11. If you notice carefully, Hebrews 12:1 says, "let us also lay aside." It is an appeal for us also to live like these heroes. In other words, these are not just examples for us to admire. This isn't just a historical heritage for us to be proud of. These are not idols for us to adore. They are not just stories to help us understand where we came from. It's much more than that. This is our invitation to run the race that has been set before us in the same way Enoch, Abel, Noah, Abraham, and Moses laid aside weights and ran.

Invited into the Book of Acts

When you read the end of the book of Acts, you'll quickly notice the story just leaves you hanging with Paul still in prison. The book has no literary conclusion. That's because the book of Acts is not complete. All other New Testament books have a closing, but not Acts. That's because the acts of the apostles continued after Luke put his pen down. And they are still continuing today. The story of the Church is still being written. How *we* live our lives determines how the rest of the book of Acts gets written. Just like we should model our lives after the early apostles, writing church history with our lives, in the same way, we should be working on adding our own names to the Hall of Faith in Hebrews 11. The Hall of Faith isn't complete yet. The writer says I don't have time to talk about all the rest of them.[21] And then he gives us an invitation in Hebrews 12 to lay aside every weight and sin which clings so closely and let us run with endurance the race that is set before us by looking to Jesus.

How we live our lives determines how the rest of the book of Acts gets written.

Hearing and Fellowship

God does not ask us to do something we cannot do. He is asking us to live like the apostles and like the heroes of faith. That can be done, but it will require real faith in God, and elevating our thinking far above the mindset of this world. As with all faith, faith to live this life comes by hearing. And sometimes we add, "by hearing and hearing and hearing," and that's okay. Faith does come that way, and it is important to continuously and consistently hear

21 Heb. 11:32

the Word of God. But no one lived a lifestyle of strong faith and only heard the Word with their natural ears. They all spent time with Jesus.

In the early church, after the lame man at the gate called Beautiful was healed, Peter and John were brought before the rulers, elders, and scribes—the very same forum who condemned Jesus to death a few months earlier. At the time Jesus was standing before the Sanhedrin, Peter was out in the courtyard and even denied knowing Jesus out of fear for his own life. But this time, Peter is on trial himself and boldly proclaimed "let it be known to all of you and to all the people of Israel that by the name of Jesus Christ of Nazareth, whom you crucified, whom God raised from the dead—by him this man is standing before you well."[22] When the rulers, "saw the boldness of Peter and John, and perceived that they were uneducated, common men, they were astonished. And they recognized that they had been with Jesus."[23]

Without strong fellowship with Jesus, there will be no strong faith life. You see, it's one thing to know the promise; to know what the written Word says. But it's another thing to know the Promisor. And in order for us to have confidence in a promise, we have to know something about the authority who gave the promise.

---

22 Acts 4:10
23 Acts 4:13

As a child, it was a lot easier to believe my father if he said he would give me a certain toy for my birthday than it was to believe a stranger who said the same thing. In order to have faith in someone's word, we have to have confidence in the trustworthiness of the individual who said it. Such confidence is built by spending time with someone, and over time seeing that they have been faithful to their promises. This is why, in order to have a strong faith life, we must both know the Word of God well, but we also must have a strong fellowship with the God of the Word. Otherwise, we don't have much to "hang our faith on" so to speak. So, as we read about and study the heroes of faith, we are supposed to imitate their faith, their obedience, and their courage. But in order to do this, we must look unto Jesus, the author and finisher of our faith. This is our invitation to lay aside some things and focus on Jesus so we can join the Hall of Faith ourselves.

James Inviting Us to This Kind of Faith

The author of Hebrews isn't the only one inviting us to the Hall of Faith. So did James, the brother of Jesus. He wrote to predominantly Jewish believers. In encouraging them on the tremendous power available in prayer, James used the example of Elijah and said, "he is a man with a nature like ours."[24]

24 James 5:17

The Jews would section the Old Testament into two parts; the law and the prophets. Moses would be the main character of the law, and Elijah would be considered the largest prophet. That's why Moses and Elijah were the ones who appeared with Jesus on the mount of transfiguration (*see* Matt. 17:3). But in teaching on prayer, James wrote:

> **The prayer of a righteous person has great power as it is working. Elijah was a man with a nature like ours, and he prayed fervently that it might not rain, and for three years and six months it did not rain on the earth. Then he prayed again, and heaven gave rain, and the earth bore its fruit.**
>
> **James 5:16b–18**

Elijah prayed alone and yet *in one prayer session*, he impacted the entire nation of Israel for three and a half years. And even though he was the largest prophet (or the biggest man of God in the mind of Jews), he was still just a man with a nature like ours. James is telling us not to put Elijah on such a pedestal that it becomes impossible in our minds to do what he did. No, James is inviting us to believe we can do the same kind of things Elijah did. He is inviting each and every one of us to be so aware of our righteousness in Christ that we go out and do tremendous things just like Elijah did.

Actually, Elijah is an Old Testament example. We have a better covenant. There ought to be stronger encounters and greater exploits among us than what we see in Hebrews 11 because we have greater promises, and we have God Himself *in us*, not just outwardly some place.

Jesus Invites Us into Greater Works

In the same way that the writer of Hebrews invites us into the Hall of Faith, Luke, who wrote the gospel of Luke and Acts, invites us to continue writing the book of Acts. Just like James invites us to make tremendous power available through prayer like Elijah did, so also Jesus invites us to go out and do greater works.

> **Truly, truly, I say to you, whoever believes in me will also do the works that I do; and greater works than these will he do, because I am going to the Father.**
>
> **John 14:12**

Much debate and discussion has been made regarding what the greater works are. For one, the greater works Jesus talks of could not be the new birth, because we are not the ones that do that. It is the Holy Spirit that regenerates people as they believe. So, at a minimum, we are to do the works of Jesus. At the same time, an example of greater work in the books of Acts would be, "so that they even carried out the sick into the streets and laid them on cots and mats, that as Peter came by at least his shadow might fall on some of them."[25] During Jesus' day, people would come to touch the hem of His garment or to touch Jesus. But during Peter's ministry, at times they weren't looking for a cloth or a touch. Just the shadow was enough. That would be an example of greater works in the ministry of Peter than there was in the ministry of Jesus.

Consciousness of Stronger Encounters

If you will start to study and meditate on the examples and scriptures you have just read, you will find that a greater awareness of these things will start to arise from within. It may not come in a day, a week, or even in a few months. But if you diligently study and meditate on these things, faith will rise, you will stir yourself up, and the gifts of God in you will come alive in such a way that you become a mighty force to be reckoned with.

Yet, sadly, I meet lots of believers and even ministers who do not have this mindset. I often hear Christians saying, "Oh, God, please be with me today." When I hear that, I immediately think, *What Bible have you read this morning? God is in me*. Somebody who's looking outwardly for

25 Acts 5:15

an answer needs to go back to the Bible and realize God is in them. I've never been anywhere where the presence of God isn't because I always bring His presence with me.

You can go into the darkest of dark places. And I have traveled to some of the darkest places on earth. As I go, I know I don't have a small light. From early childhood, we were taught the song, "This little light of mine, I'm gonna let it shine." No, no, no, no, no, no! The Creator of the heavens and the earth lives on the inside of me. I carry Him everywhere I go. I do not have a little light in me. The great I AM is on the inside, and that is the light I allow to shine everywhere I go. I have been to areas infested by witch doctors, I have been to areas infiltrated by Al Shabaab terrorists, and I once traveled into the Congo while an Ebola outbreak was happening.

One time I took two police officers with me and traveled in the border region between Kenya and Somalia. The road from Garissa through Bura, Hola, and on to Garsen was very poorly maintained at the time and large sections of it were nothing more than wheel ruts in the sand. In addition, it was also notorious for bandits, so very few people would even travel this road. I knew we had

I've never been anywhere where the presence of God isn't because I always bring His presence with me.

work to do in these areas, so I spent extra time rereading Psalm 23, Psalm 91, and meditating on God's promises of protection. As we went, we encountered bandits alongside the road. I will never forget the fear in the faces of those armed police officers in my car when we saw them. But I kept focusing on the joy and the peace of God that I had in my heart, and we just kept going. No harm came near us that day. We just kept driving.

So, meditate on the truth that the fullness of Christ is in us.[26] I can share that I have studied and meditated on this power available to us who believe. Regarding prayer and the power available to us, I studied and meditated on how Abraham, Moses, Elijah, and others cooperated with this power in prayer. Over time, the prayer assignments have gotten bigger and bigger. In prayer, several times I have been to places where international geopolitical decisions are made.

Back in 2010 and 2011, we spent quite some time praying for Somalia. The country had been under anarchy since the early 1990s and was a very difficult place for the Gospel to get in. Over the years, American forces, Europeans, and the African Union had at various times tried to bring order and stability to the nation, but without much success. This was also the time of the international crisis with the Somali pirates operating in international waters along the coast of Africa.

---

26 Col. 2:9–10

In the early fall of 2011, I was in Malindi, Kenya. I was walking the shores, looking out at the Indian Ocean where the pirates were, and I started praying. An earnest, heartfelt prayer came upon me. In the Spirit, I sensed that international forces were to enter Somalia from the south and liberate the country as far north as to Mogadishu, affecting roughly the southern half of the country. I simply prayed out what I saw, and only a few weeks later, Kenyan Defence Forces launched Operation Linda Nchi, and things transpired exactly the way I had prayed them. Today, Somali refugees are returning to Somalia, starting businesses, foreign investors are setting up banks, and daily commercial flights are going into Mogadishu. When there is peace and prosperity in a nation, it is also easier to bring the Gospel. There is still much more to be done, but the power available to us in prayer truly does affect nations.

But we don't get to those places just by reading this book. You'll have to study the Scriptures and meditate on these truths until that kind of thinking becomes part of your being. Our faith must grow to where we not only believe it is possible, but that we truly expect such things to happen.

This is an invitation for us to live our lives in such a way that at the end of our life, it's an example that belongs in Hebrews chapter 11. What were these people like?

Traits of Those in the Hall of Faith

As we consider the invitation for each of us to join the Hall of Faith, we know we also will have a race to run and we will have to lay aside some things. Let's ask the questions, "What were the traits of the people of faith in Hebrews 11 and what did they have in common?" This will help us see how to run this race and what it will cost us.

Assignments Bigger Than Themselves

In reading through Hebrews 11, you can quickly notice that none of the stories made it in because of their quest for personal success. Even though Abraham and David had great personal wealth, this isn't mentioned or even alluded to in the faith chapter. What we do see is people accomplishing assignments bigger than themselves and their own family. The story of Noah isn't just that of a man who saved his own life, but it is about one who followed God and thereby had an impact on the whole world. Moses is another example. He chose to lay down his personal wealth, the treasures of Egypt, in order that he might help save his people.

Today, many people have million-dollar-home dreams, and that's wonderful. We have been promised to be the head and not the tail financially, and the Lord will prosper what we put our hand to do. At the same time, there is a big problem when our own personal wealth and well being is at the top of our wish lists and dream boards. That's called selfishness. This life is not about us. It's about something that is greater. The heroes of faith had assignments that were bigger than themselves and their families. And they became an inspiration for others to follow. They set examples and they set precedents. All of them. Let us live like them and not chase the dreams and methods the world would consider success.

Walked Contrary to Mainstream

People of great faith do not think and live like ordinary people. They spend time with God and allow God's thoughts to influence their lives. They think and act differently to people of the world and even other believers who are too influenced by the world. All the heroes of faith walked contrary to their peers and the mainstream around them. For example, Enoch walked so closely with God that he became the first person to be raptured, stepping right over into the presence of God. And while the world had evil thoughts continually, Noah walked with God and faithfully worked year after year after year building the ark. Ordinarily, one would have given up after a while, working on a project year after year that no one else around them believes in. But Noah was convinced of what God said, not what others were thinking. Abel walked differently from the few people that were around him at that

> People of great faith do not think and live like ordinary people. They spend time with God and allow God's thoughts to influence their lives.

time, and his brother rose up in jealousy because of the sin that was in his own life. Moses' parents hid him for months, because they were not afraid of Pharaoh's edict. This was during the time when most other young boys perished. Even the prostitute Rahab did something different from everybody around her. Why? Because she was convinced of something bigger than the people around her were convinced about.

All these heroes had to be so convinced of the things of God, that what others around them thought and did made no difference to them. Their lives became examples and they set precedent for us to follow. It just isn't possible to live life being overly concerned about the opinions of those around us and still walk in faith of what God said. Often, what God tells someone to do may be so out of the ordinary that even others who know God and walk by faith themselves would discourage that person from doing what God told them to do.

> **Let us leave the elementary doctrine of Christ and go on to maturity, not laying again a foundation of … faith towards God.**
>
> **Hebrews 6:1**

We should strive to live a life of faith that goes beyond just believing God for our own personal salvation and our own personal promises. Thank God for salvation and the other things He promised us. We need those things. But let's go beyond focusing on things purely for ourselves to focusing on the assignments God has for us. Those assignments will come from Him and will require you to be willing to walk contrary to many people around you. This does not mean to be weird for the sake of being different, but rather to be so convinced of what God has called you to do, that you don't mind what others may think of you.

Close Fellowship to God

But there is something that is more, there is something that is beyond. All of the people from Hebrews 11 had assignments that required them to walk so close to God, they were able to hear His voice in the face of very challenging situations. Your assignment is the same way! My assignment is the same way! And the further I walk with God, often the assignments get more challenging. Sometimes the assignments get more peculiar. Sometimes the assignment is so different, I don't have an example to follow of someone who has had a similar assignment.

Over the years, we have opened a number of Bible colleges, and customary business sense would tell us to standardize all of the operations so that expansion becomes easier. We do standardize, but not so rigid that we cannot hear from God. In Northeastern Kenya, a particularly challenging area where we could not find anyone doing any significant Christian work, we struggled to find a way to effectively reach the people. We kept praying for effective laborers to be sent there. While we could not find a way to get it done, we had a government official of Kenya come to us and explain that he had security workers stationed in the area. The laws of Kenya allowed for some of those government security officers to function as chaplains, but he needed someone to train them. So we designed a unique training program specifically for them. As a result, they became effective in helping the people in those difficult regions to receive the Gospel. We have received many testimonies of churches being opened in areas that have never had any churches because of our willingness to be flexible and listen to God in every situation. These unique assignments cannot be planned, but answers come out of strong fellowship with God and learning how to listen to Him.

Let's look at the example of Isaac, but first we need to understand who his father, Abraham, was. Abraham was not only Isaac's natural dad, but he was also *the* great example of faith. Even today, Jews, Christians, and Muslims, which combined are more than 50 percent of the world population, consider Abraham their father. In addition, Abraham was also a great businessman. We know from Scripture he had at least 318 people who were trained soldiers working for him. In total, his business operation must have had over 1,000 employees if he had that many soldiers.

In Genesis 26, we find Isaac shortly after his father Abraham had passed away. After his father's death, Isaac encountered a famine in the land similar to the famine his father Abraham had experienced. Abraham went through several famines and showed Isaac by example that during famine, you go and look for pasture elsewhere. Once he went to Abimelech of the Philistines. Another time he went down to Egypt. So Isaac was pondering going down to Egypt, following in the footsteps of his father Abraham, when the Lord told him:

> **Do not go down to Egypt; dwell in the land of which I shall tell you. Sojourn in this land, and I will be with you and will bless you…**
>
> **Genesis 26:2–3**

Looking at natural circumstances and conventional wisdom, it would make sense to go to Egypt. Abraham had shown him by example that in this case, going to Egypt would be a good thing. But the Lord told Isaac differently.

Here, God's instruction doesn't make any sense to reason. But Isaac obeyed and he settled in Gerar, contrary to the example of faith that had been given him.

> **And Isaac sowed in that land and reaped in the same year a hundredfold. The Lord blessed him, and the man became rich and gained more and more until he became very wealthy.**
>
> **Genesis 26:12–13**

It's actually a very interesting aside that Isaac's hundredfold return was not because of giving to Melchisedek, the priest, in a church offering or giving to the work of God. What he did, in modern day language, was invest into his own business. Now, there are principles of sowing and reaping and we can learn from them. But in this instance, Isaac got instructions from God and did exactly like he was told. He did something contrary to what normal voices would have said to do in this particular situation. He invested in his own business when everything in the natural was saying, "It's time to get out." And the Lord liked it. And the man became rich because the Lord blessed him. God blesses good business. Isaac had to be in close fellowship with God to not only know His voice but to trust what he was told. Isaac is in the Hall of Faith not just because he listened closely to God regarding staying in Gerar, but he had the courage to expand when natural circumstances were telling him to be careful.

Through close fellowship with God, we are able to hear His instructions for us. And they are not always going to be aligned with conventional wisdom. In fact, it is a common trait of everyone in Hebrews 11 that at times they had to follow God's instructions, which put them at odds with conventional wisdom.

Likewise, in today's age and mentality, we have become accustomed to having a success and a growth mindset. We often push in growing from level to level in our churches, businesses, and organizations. For example, a church will often grow to 200 or 300 members, and it takes a lot of passion, energy, and perseverance to start a new work and grow it to that level. Typically, the pastor will then start asking what changes are needed in order to grow from 300 to 1,000. Frequently, growing to the next level is good, but that might not always be the case, so we have to get the instructions from the Lord. Every church on earth is not called to become a megachurch. In some ways, if the Lord tells the pastor that continued numerical growth isn't the goal, it may be harder to listen and follow than to do what others expect ought to be done. I know of a number of pastors that do excellent multiplying many smaller churches instead of focusing on growing a large megachurch.

Unless we stay in close fellowship with Him, we are destined to make the mistake of following the crowds or conventional wisdom, and we will miss the individual instructions He gives us concerning our lives, our call, and our assignments.

More Than Copying Actions

In the example of Isaac, we saw how he could not just copy the example of his father, even though Abraham's faith is a model for us to follow. We are to imitate and learn from other's faith, but we do not simply copy their actions.

> **By faith the people crossed the Red Sea as if on dry land, but the Egyptians, when they attempted to do the same, were drowned.**
>
> **Hebrews 11:29**

The Egyptians tried to copy the actions of Moses and they drowned. Similarly, the seven sons of Sceva tried to cast out demons by just copying what Paul did, and that didn't end well for them.[27] Faith is not about copying actions. Faith is about knowing God so well that your actions come out of personal conviction, not what somebody else has done. We don't copy actions. We get our own instructions from heaven.

27 Acts 19:11–20

Too many have missed God by looking to others, seeing what they are doing, and just copying them. Just because another church is doing very well running a school is no sign that your church should be running a school. Just because another evangelist decided to become a pastor and start a church is no sign that you have been called to start a church. Likewise, in business, just because the trends and the analysts are all talking about a certain kind of new development in your industry does not always mean your business should go the same direction. God may have another niche and another path for you. I know of a number of business people who are beating their competition because they get their wisdom from God and know how to hear His voice. You need to stay close to Him so you can get those specific directions from Him.

Faith is not about copying actions. Faith is about knowing God so well that your actions come out of personal conviction

Strong Opposition

Another common trait of the heroes of faith is they encountered strong opposition. They all had to know God in such a way that they lived by their convictions no matter what difficulties they faced. They were going to follow God "come hell or high water," so to speak. It didn't matter the circumstances. It didn't matter how strong the opposition was.

Can you imagine Noah? I don't know how long it took him to build the ark, but I am quite sure he didn't order it from a shipyard. He didn't have anyone on his team except for his three sons and their wives. He may very well have had to cut trees and saw the lumber himself. Regardless of the details, the project was huge and most would agree that it took him many decades, maybe as many as 100 years to build the ark.

The voices against him must have been very, very strong each and every day. I can't imagine he didn't question himself and ask, "What am I doing?" As with any such project and not many people supporting you, there would have been plenty of opportunities to quit. But his conviction was so strong he ended up in Hebrews 11.

Surrounded by challenging situations, how do we listen? When those voices are loud, when well-meaning friends give us advice contrary to what God said, then what do we do? Well-meaning friends and good advice from godly counsel is beneficial. There is safety in being surrounded by good people. But there's also a place we *must* get to where we know the assignment in our heart is burning in such a way that it doesn't matter what people are saying. It only matters what God said.

Risked Their Life for the Assignment

In Hebrews 11, I find a group of people who took great personal risks to follow God. They chose to live by their convictions—live or die, sink or swim. They put their trust in God and they did not hold their own lives dear, nor did they fear people. They simply followed God no matter the cost. They were not afraid of risking their own personal comfort in order to serve a larger cause. To really be a pioneer or to accomplish something remarkable, one of the most important things you have to get rid of is fear. Most all fear is rooted in the fear of death, but for the believer, death is nothing to be afraid of. Meditating on the realities of heaven, the realities of the presence of God, and thinking about the fact that the things of God are more real than the temporary things of the earth will help us to put things in proper perspective and will help us walk fearlessly on this earth. It will help us develop the attitude of Sabina Wurmbrand. The Wurmbrands worked in Communist Romania, and her husband, Richard, was tortured by the regime for his faith and work with the Gospel. Later on, they founded the organization, The Voice of the Martyrs. When faced with the possibility of her husband becoming a martyr for his faith, she replied, "I would rather be a widow than be married to a coward."

No, I am not looking to become a martyr, and I am nowhere near suicidal. At the same time, I am not afraid of dying. In fact, at every believer's funeral, I don't sorrow for the person who has passed on. I choose to remember where they are and a part of me longs to be where they are, because it is so much better there than it is here. So I am not afraid, and I refuse to let any kind of fear hold me back from doing what God has called me to do. Really, the worst someone can do to us is send us to walk on streets of gold a little bit earlier than we had planned. When you stop and think about it, that's not too bad, is it?

They Just Did the Right Thing

Before we wrap up the traits of the heroes from Hebrews 11, there are many more characteristics I could mention and expound upon, but I want to focus on just one more. Though they are famous now, their decisions of obedience at the time was not a search for fame. Abel did not know he would end up in the Hall of Faith. He just did what was right at the moment. Consider David. As a teenager,[28] he was shepherding the sheep of his father. That was an entry-level job. But even doing an entry-level job, David lived in such a way that he did the right thing, and what could be considered "above and beyond," even when no one was watching. When a lion or bear tried to take one of the sheep he was shepherding, he rescued it and killed the lion or bear. That's going beyond expectations if you ask me. He could have grown bitter working so hard with

28 We do not know David's exact age, but he most likely was a teenager.

such a "small assignment," but he continued to do the right thing with such a menial task. His brothers even looked down on him and his job. And then one day Samuel the prophet came and called everyone to a feast. David's dad, Jesse, didn't even consider inviting David to the biggest party they'd ever had, but left him tending the sheep. The big prophet Samuel had come and the event was bigger than our modern Christmas, Easter, or a family wedding. David could have easily been offended for not being invited to this major event, but he wasn't. He did the right thing. And that's where David started, just doing what was right regardless of who noticed or what others thought. And like many others in Hebrews 11, that is one of the attitudes that propelled them to be included in the Hall of Faith.

These are the heroes who ran their races well. With big tasks ahead, they went contrary to the mainstream. They knew their God and walked according to His voice regardless of opposition. No matter the risk, they focused on doing what was right. This is the group of people we have been invited to be part of, joining in with this great cloud of witnesses.

CHAPTER THREE

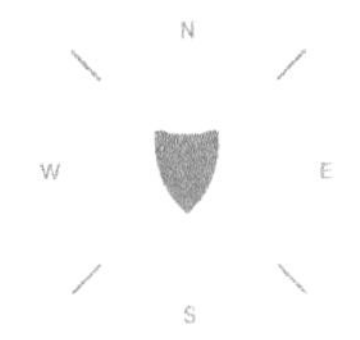

The Lost Story of Terah

Ur—An Advanced Society

The story of Abraham's father, Terah, is a remarkable one. He is the one who started the journey with his family, which is the journey Abraham later became famous for, leaving Ur and heading for Canaan's land. When Terah and Abraham left Ur, it was the largest city in the world at the time. In comparison with today, they would have left Tokyo, New York City, Paris, Nairobi, or some place like that. While this was almost 4,000 years ago, the Mesopotamians had built an advanced society, and Terah's origin was very different from the nomadic lifestyle of the Canaanites.

Ur was a very well developed port city, a trade center where the general population was bilingual. About 80 percent of the population of the area lived in the city, meaning only 20 percent were rural or farmers. The ratio of urban to rural population is one of the quickest ways to see how developed a society is. Generally speaking, the rural population is involved with farming or food production, while the urban population have moved on from the primary trades to other industries. The more efficient food production is, the more that society can be involved in advancing other areas and industries. Looking at the modern world today, the continent of Africa has a population that is 50 percent urban and 50 percent rural. In 1970, the United States' urban population was only 73 percent, and the country did not reach the urbanization level of Ur until about the year 2010.[29] Similarly, Europe had an urbanization rate of 62 percent in 1970 which rose to 75 percent by 2020.[30, 31]

At the time of Terah and Abraham, the city was almost 2,000 years old and had extensive infrastructure with roads, irrigation, and water canals. Houses were often two story villas, could have 10 to 15 rooms, and were made with bricks and plastered walls. They even invented an early form of air conditioning. During the hot season, they would channel the cool river water into canals underneath the houses that would then cool down the buildings.

---

29 US Census bureau and/or Urban Percentage of the Population for States, Historical | Iowa Community Indicators Program (https://www.icip.iastate.edu/tables/population/urban-pct-states)
30 European Union Urban Population 1960-2023 | MacroTrends (https://www.macrotrends.net/global-metrics/countries/EUU/european-union/urban-population)
31 Note: There are variations in definitions of urban versus rural and in the data past 1900. The point the author is making is not in the accuracy of the data past 1900, but rather that the modern world didn't have the urbanization rates of Ur until far past the year 1900. In the timeline of world history, Ur was very advanced.

They were also advanced in academics and education. The population was bilingual, speaking both Sumarian and Akkadian. The world's oldest written laws are from Ur. At Mari, one of the other influential cities of the empire, archaeologists found a library with 22,000 tablets. There are even indications there was a postal system during the time of Abraham.[32]

Dear Reader: You can see pictures of the temple and houses from Ur in Chaldea at safarimission.org/books/faithforassignments or by scanning the QR code.

On this webpage, you will also find a picture of an excavated and restored house that archaeologists have named "Abraham's house." It's an example of the huge houses found in Ur, and shows that Abraham had a very different upbringing from the tents he lived in for the rest of his life.

32 You can study more about the Mesopotamians in any standard work on World History, or you can use Wikipedia's articles on 'Ur' as a starting point. To align with the time period of Abraham, look into the Bronze Age, or approximately the year 2000 BC.

State Controlled Religion in a World Empire

At the center of Ur was a huge ziggurat, a pyramid-looking structure that served as a temple for the moon-god Nanna. This ziggurat towered over all other buildings in the city. In Mesopotamia, government and religion were intertwined, and the king often served as the chief priest as well. All of society—the government, commerce, and arts—were affected by this worldview, and the temple at the ziggurat was the focal point of it all. There was no room for the worship of God Almighty. Throughout history, empires have always tried to control religion, sought to exclude worship of the one true God, and worked to expand globally. This is the story in Babel, Mesopotamia, Egypt, the Greek and Roman empires, and down to modern times with the Nazis and the Communists. The spirit of Antichrist has long been at work, and there are many in elitist circles today working on creating a one world global godless society.

In times like these, God frequently calls individuals out from such situations. At other times, He has called His people to stay in order to be salt and light in difficult circumstances. During Nazi times, Dietrich Bonhoffer said, "Silence in the face of evil is itself evil. God will not hold us guiltless. Not to speak is to speak. Not to act is to act."[33]

---

33 Metaxas, Eric. "Bonhoffer: Pastor, Martyr, Prophet, Spy" 2010. Quote is on the book jacket. Some have questioned the authenticity of the quote, even though it summarizes well how Bonhoffer lived.

Bonhoffer boldly moved back to Germany in order to be a voice and help the Church there during very difficult times.

In his book, *This World: Playground or Battleground?* A.W. Tozer wrote, "A scared world needs a fearless church. Surely, Bible-reading Christians should be the last persons on earth to give way to hysteria. They are redeemed from their past offenses, kept in their present circumstances by the power of an all-powerful God, and their future is safe in His hands. God has promised to support them in the flood, protect them in the fire, feed them in the famine, shield them against their enemies, hide them in His safe chambers … and receive them at last into eternal tabernacles … Surely, a fear-ridden Christian has never examined His defenses. A fear-stricken church cannot help a scared world … We'll never convince a scared world that there is peace at the cross if we continue to exhibit the same fears as those who make no profession of Christianity."

In New Testament times, we are generally called to be in the world, even though we are not of it, in order to be salt and light. Generally speaking, under the Old Testament, God told His people to separate from the world so they would not be corrupted by the world. But in the New Testament, God put His Spirit within us and empowered us to be an influence to those around us. We are to take of the life, love, and presence of God that He has poured out in our hearts, to take a piece of heaven and give it to those around us. Yet, even though, generally speaking, we are to be in the world in order to be an influence, there may also be times when God gives specific instructions to get out of certain situations. One time, the Apostle Paul escaped through the city wall in a basket,[34] and Jesus also hid Himself for a season because of imminent danger.[35]

In the case of Terah, consider that he came from a place that was very well advanced technologically, was a well developed society, but had the problem of an evil state controlled religion.

The Story of Terah

Now that we know Terah came from an amazingly advanced civilization—one with a lot of conveniences available, but also evil rulers who built a society where the worship of God was not allowed—let's look closer at Terah and his journey in life.

Terah had three sons in Ur—Abram, Nahor, and Haran. Haran fathered Lot, but later died "in the presence of his Father Terah in the land of his kindred, in Ur of the Chaldeans."[36]

Joshua explained, "Long ago, your fathers lived beyond the Euphrates, Terah, the father of Abraham and of

34 Acts 9:24-25
35 John 7:1, John 11:53-54
36 Gen. 11:28

Nahor; and they served other gods."[37] Apparently, Terah's family was well integrated into society and served the moon-God Nanna like the rest of civilization.

Later, Terah left Ur with Abram and Sarai, one of his sons and daughter in law, as well as his grandson, Lot. Terah's other living son at the time, Nahor, did not go with them. The Bible does not say why Nahor didn't come, but the most probable explanation is Nahor was not willing to forsake his culture and religion for the sake of following God.

At any rate, the rest of the family left Ur and set out to go to the land of Canaan. This meant they set out to leave the entire Mesopotamian empire to go to a land that was uncivilized, settled by the nomadic Canaanites.

> **But when they came to Haran, they settled there.**
>
> **Genesis 11:31**

Haran is at the edge of the Mesopotamian empire. They'd made the decision to leave Ur and go to Canaan's land. Leaving Ur must have taken quite some courage; packing up all their belongings and leaving the most comfortable city on earth. Terah's resolve was strong enough that he was willing to leave part of his family behind if they were not willing to go with him, which is exactly what hap-

37 Josh. 24:2

pened with Nahor, and the Bible has nothing more to say about him. Terah's other son, Haran, had already passed away. We don't know, but it might be that Terah named the settlement at the edge of the Mesopotamian empire after his deceased son.

While Terah and his family undoubtedly went through quite an experience in order to get to Haran, Haran was never intended to be their destination. But since Haran geographically was at the edge of the Mesopotamian empire, it would mean that in order to travel any further, they would have to give up even more things. Going further would mean leaving civilization completely and going into an area where nomads lived. It would mean leaving even more convenience and start mingling with a people whose language, culture, and way of life was very different from what they were used to. Those would naturally be hard and uncomfortable decisions to make. And after all, they had already made lots of uncomfortable choices to get to where they were, so instead of making further sacrifices, "they settled there."

And from here, the Bible really has nothing more to say about Terah, except that he died at an age of 205 years old.[38] The only other mention of Terah in the Bible is Joshua's reference to Terah and Abraham coming from Ur where they served foreign gods, and Terah is naturally mentioned in genealogies.

---

38 Gen. 11:32

Terah did not make it into the Hall of Faith in Hebrews 11. Why? All of the ones listed in Hebrews 11 finished their course or their assignments. Hebrews 10:38 says, "but my righteous one shall live by faith, and if he shrinks back, my soul has no pleasure in him."

Faith perseveres. Faith is patient. Faith keeps believing God when it looks impossible. Concluding the Hall of Faith, we read "let us run with endurance the race that is set before us."[39]

Let us remember back to Jesus walking on the water, and Peter walking on the water towards Him. Peter did walk on the water. It wasn't until he changed his focus and started to look at the waves, the wind, and the challenging circumstances that he started to sink. As long as he focused on the word Jesus spoke, "Come," and stayed focused on his target, which was going to Jesus, he walked on the water just fine. But so many people today get distracted along the way and allow the circumstances of life to get them into fear and worry. After Jesus lifted Peter up and they got back into the boat, Jesus gave him a very valuable lesson. In our natural minds, we would think Peter should be commended. After all, he was the only one who had the

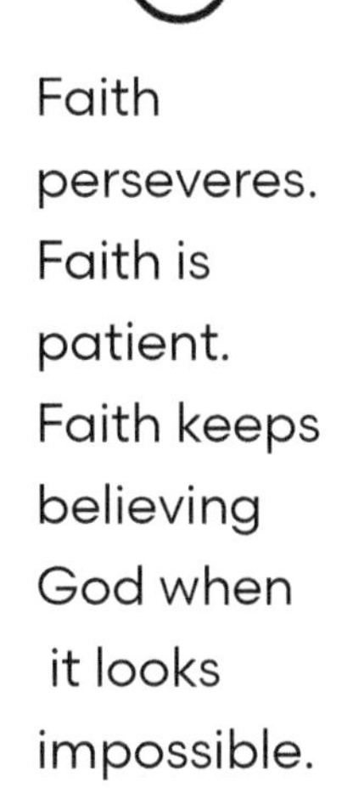

39 Heb. 12:2

courage to get out of the boat. But instead, Jesus asked, "O you of little faith, why did you doubt?"[40]

God expects us to walk by faith and finish the course set before us. There would have been no story of Noah if he would have quit along the way. Moses would have been unknown if he quit in the wilderness when the whole nation was complaining against him.

Terah Was the One Who Was Called

When we look back at Terah in the book of Genesis, there is something very interesting and important to understand. The book of Genesis has natural chapters or divisions. The writer kept on using the same phrase, "These are the generations of …" when introducing the next section of the book. The phrase, "These are the generations of …" appears a number of times and each time it introduces a new section or the next main character. Consider carefully the following listing:

> **These are the generations of the heavens and the earth when they were created …**
>
> **Genesis 2:4**

40 Matt. 14:31

This is the book of the generations of Adam.

Genesis 5:1

These are the generations of Noah.

Genesis 6:9

These are the generations of the sons of Noah, Shem, Ham, and Japheth.

Genesis 10:1

These are the generations of Shem.

Genesis 11:10

These are the generations of Terah.

Genesis 11:27

These are the generations of Isaac.

Genesis 25:19

These are the generations of Esau.

Genesis 36:1

These are the generations of Jacob.

Genesis 37:2

Here we have the natural divisions of the book of Genesis. The divisions are: creation of heavens and the earth; Adam; Noah; the sons of Noah, Terah; Isaac; Esau; Jacob.

Interestingly enough, this outline is very similar to the listing of the heroes of the Hall of Faith in Hebrews 11. But in the division of Genesis, there is somebody who really seems to be missing. There is no inscription in the book of Genesis, "These are the generations of Abraham." And yet Abraham is the father of over 50 percent of the world population today. Christians, Jews, and Muslims all consider him their father, either spiritually or naturally. In many ways it could be argued that Abraham is the most influential historical figure in the book. Yet, Genesis is lacking the division, "These are the generations of Abraham." Why? Because it says, "These are the generations of Terah." That's Abraham's father. Everything the book of Genesis shares about Abraham and Sarah falls under the division about Terah. It was Terah who originally left Ur for the purpose of going into Canaan's land. Terah had a purpose. He had an assignment from God to get out from underneath state religion, to get out from under the one world empire kind of mentality. And the assignment was to go into Canaan's land. Terah started out well. He did like Peter, he stepped out of the boat and started walking on the water. But at some point he started to doubt, he settled down, and accepted less than what his calling was.

Faith Isn't Trying

We need to ask Terah like Jesus asked Peter, "Why did you doubt?" He was not commended for trying. Jesus simply asked, "Why did you doubt?" I am utterly convinced Abraham was not the one who received the call. His father was. And I believe that's why there is no inscription, "These are the generations of Abraham." We only find "These are the generations of Terah." Terah started out well. He stepped out of the boat and started walking in his assignments. He did that until the assignment became too big for him, and he was not willing to sacrifice comfort in order to fulfill what God called him to do. After that, the Bible says nothing more about Terah, except when Joshua referred to Terah's family saying, "they served other gods."[41] Apart from this mention by Joshua and being included in a couple of genealogies, the Bible has nothing more to say about Terah after he quit and settled down. But he started out, and he started well. But faith for assignments requires you not to just start, but to finish.

The Apostle Paul encouraged Timothy along these lines and described the persistent, dedicated life willing to sacrifice comfort in order to focus on a goal.

> **No soldier gets entangled in civilian pursuits, since his aim is to please the one who enlisted him. An athlete is not crowned unless**

41 Josh. 24:2

he competes according to the rules. It is the hard-working farmer who ought to have the first share of the crops.

2 Timothy 4:4–6

Soldiers, athletes, and farmers are all careers that require training, persistence, hard work, and, maybe most of all, a focused dedication until you reach the end goal. The soldier can't quit in the middle of the battle when the heat is on. The athlete running the marathon gets no recognition unless the last mile is finished. And the farmer must see his work through until the harvest has been gathered into the barn.

Commendable faith does not start out walking on the water and then quit. It does not set out to reach the land of Canaan and settle along the way. Maybe you, dear reader, have slowed down or quit the assignment God gave you. But with God, there is hope, mercy, and grace. If you have slowed down or even quit along the way, decide today to begin again and God will help you get back up and get back on track. Thank God, Peter did learn and ended up finishing his race well.

Throughout history and even amongst our own contemporaries, many have gone as far as the price that they were willing to pay—halfway. We need to be of the mindset of the writer of Hebrews when he said, "But we are not of those who shrink back and are destroyed, but of those who have faith and preserve their souls."[42] We have a great commission. There is a lost, dying, and hurting world, and we need to do what is necessary in order to reach them. We're in a race and it needs to be finished.

Abraham Finished His Assignments

While Terah quit along the way, his son Abraham did not. (Note: Abram is the same person as Abraham. He changed his name later in life as we will see in a bit.) All throughout his life, he kept on taking new assignments. Just consider this brief timeline with a few highlights:

At 75 years old, Abram left his father in Haran. They had walked with God together from Ur, but now that Terah won't go further, Abram stepped out with his wife and nephew, and they set out to do what God had previously destined for the family.[43] Sometimes we will be called to do what others should have done but have left undone.

---

42 Heb. 10:39

43 When you read Gen. 11:32, it seems as though Terah died in Haran before Abraham left Haran in Gen. 12:4. Note that all details in Scripture are not chronological as we are used to telling stories. Rather, the Bible finished the story of Terah in Gen. 11:32 so that it can fully focus on Abraham from Gen. 12:1. We know this, because according to Gen. 12:4, Abraham was 75 years old when he left Haran. And Terah was 70 years old when Abraham was born (Gen. 11:26). This means that Terah was 145 years old when Abraham left Haran. Terah then lived another 60 years and died at the age of 205, long after Abraham, his son, left Haran.

Sometime later, Abram and Lot were so blessed that the land couldn't support both of them. Though he is the senior, Abram was generous and let Lot take the first pick of the land. Lot ought to have deferred to his elder, but instead went where it all looked good. Lot got into trouble and was taken captive by five kings who carried him off with all of his belongings, livestock, and people. But even though Lot had dishonored Abram, Abram still risked his own life in order to rescue Lot. He took 318 of his armed men and pursued the five kings, overpowered them, and restored everything to Lot. Those who walk with God will always take risks in order to help other people.

Later, when Abram was 99 years old, he still did not have his promised son. At that time, God told him to change his name from Abram to Abraham. These were Hebrew names that everyone around him understood their meaning. He now had to make announcements and tell everyone to no longer call him "Blessed Father" but to call him "Father of a Multitude." Abraham could have chosen to settle. He could have just accepted that Ishmael would be the best. What would people think and say if he changed his name? With 318 armed men, it is hard to believe he had less than 1,000 employees. Can you imagine that Monday morning when he went to his 1,000 employees and said, "You know what, guys? I just changed my name this weekend. From Blessed Father to Father of a Multitude." Can you imagine the talk going on between the employees? They probably laughed and said, "This guy is getting old. His mind must be failing. Why would you call yourself Father of a Multitude when that is impossible?" But Abraham was walking out assignments, and after he announced his name change, it was only a few months later that Sarah was pregnant. There is no such thing as plateauing. In our faith, there is always another assignment. There is always further to go. There is always more to do.

> There is no such thing as plateauing. In our faith, there is always another assignment. There is always further to go. There is always more to do.

Abraham did not stop following God once his long promised son was born. Years later, when Abraham was perhaps 115 or 125 years old, God asked him the hardest thing of his life when He told him to sacrifice his son. Yet, when God asked for his son, Isaac, Abraham still believed God and counted him able to raise Isaac from the dead. It is never too late to serve God. It is never too late to get back up. And it is never time to stop walking by faith.

CHAPTER FOUR

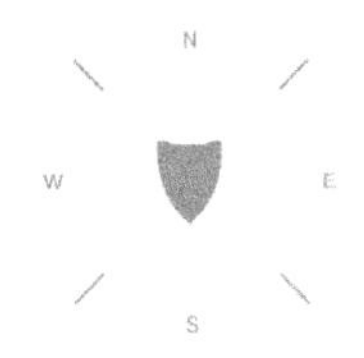

Modern Day Faith Assignments

Pastoring in the Golden Years

At our Rhema Bible Training College campus in Malindi, we had a student named John Wesley. He was in his mid 80s, the oldest student in the school, and had been a deacon in his church for 50 years. John Wesley had a sharp mind, was very engaged in the school, and as he was listening, his faith was built. After he graduated, he went to his bishop and explained that he was now trained and was ready to take on pastoring a church. Over in a rural village, the bishop had a church that really needed some help. It had gone through strife, turmoil, and church splits and there were only about a dozen people left. Now, in his upper 80s, John Wesley took on the church and started working in this village. In less than a year, he had over 200 people coming to this church!

God does not call everyone to pastor or to take a new job in their 80s, but He always has something for us to do and those who walk with God will always be ready to take on His assignments.

Reaching the Hard Areas

Another one of our graduates in Kenya is Samson Kisemei. He is from one of the most affluent families in the Maasai tribe. The Maasai tribe is a very traditional, well known African tribe in Kenya and Tanzania. The Maasai are traditionally nomadic, cattle and sheep herding, and often on the move towards better water and greener pastures. Samson's grandfather was offered to be the chief of the entire tribe. That's how influential his family is.

While his tribe is traditionally nomadic, Samson is well educated, well traveled in many places around the world, and can integrate well in the civilized world. But he sees his own people and knows they need help. So he'll go out in a very, very rural village where there has never been a church and start one. His wife is a schoolteacher and will get involved in educating the children, sometimes starting a primary school. And they've done this in community after community. Samson has started over 50 churches. And he started those in many communities where other pastors in the area had given up because this tribe is known for being very hard to reach. You don't ever find a Maasai crying. They are warriors and the rite of passage for a young Maasai is to take out a lion by yourself with a spear. If you can't do that, you can't be a man. That's just the way the tribe is. In this environment, Samson started 50 churches and has several times been beaten up by his own people for sharing the Gospel.

One day, Samson came to me and said, "I feel like my assignment is done. I've been all over these areas and established churches everywhere." What typically happens when you go into a place of utter darkness like that, and you establish a work for the Lord, other people start seeing it's possible. Then they show up and start doing other things that were too hard to do, because you showed them it's possible. These are the kind of pioneers that the people of faith are supposed to be.

Samson has been a pioneer like that, but then he came to me and asked, "Do you have some harder place to work?" I shared with him about the campus that we have near the Somalia border, where we have to gather intelligence sometimes to figure out where Al Shabaab (Al Qaeda's African sister organization) is to see whether we can get into certain towns or villages. In these areas, we have trained up many in the Kenyan military police that are stationed throughout the Somali border region, and several of these police officers have opened up public churches in these remote, hard, and volatile areas. I told Samson about the work in these areas, and he responded, "Yeah, I've been to those places. But you know, we have a military presence out there. It is not that bad. Do you have a harder place to work?"

So, Samson ended up going with us into some of the war-torn parts of the Eastern Congo, areas that have been ravaged by war and militia armies for decades. Despite very challenging circumstances and many horrific war stories among the people there, the work in Congo has continued for years with pastors seminars, radio broadcasts, and helping the people build small businesses to sustain themselves and their communities.

Think about Samson's commitment. I often wonder, *Where are those people in the world today? Where are those people in our churches?* Because these are the kind of people that belong in the Hall of Faith. This is the kind of mentality we are supposed to exemplify for other people around us.

Settling Down or Pressing In?

We have already seen how Terah settled down. Are we going to be like Terah or are we going to be like Abraham? After Terah decided to settle down in Haran, God said to Abram, "Go from your country and your kindred and your father's house to the land I will show you."[44] From here, Abram walked with God, gave the best land to Lot, later rescued Lot, received the covenant, and changed his

44 Gen. 12:1

name from Abram to Abraham. At the age of 100, Isaac was born. It now seemed like his life was complete. This would be a great time for him to settle down and focus on raising his promised child.

But then, when Isaac was between 10 and 20 years of age—we don't know exactly how old Isaac was, but we do know it was way past what we would consider time for retirement for Abraham, who could have been up to 120 years old—God tapped him on the shoulder and told him He wanted him to sacrifice Isaac, the most dear thing he had. So Abraham went on a three-day journey to Mount Moriah, which is today's Jerusalem. There, almost 2,000 years before Christ, he made an example for what Christ did for us at the cross. Abraham was willing to make such a sacrifice, long beyond when he should have settled down.

I have observed people everywhere, whether in New York City, the fjords of Norway, the affluent sides of Nairobi, the slums outside Mombasa, or the rural villages of Africa. Pastors will start a church, and it's tough work. I've pioneered many things myself, so trust me, I understand what I'm saying when I say, "Pioneering is not easy." There are numerous sacrifices. There's sweat. There are tears. There are countless challenges. There are all kinds of things you encounter. And that church will often grow to about 200 people or so. At that point there is enough income in the church where the pastor can live somewhat comfortably. The pastor no longer needs to do the heavy sacrifices to survive, so they start settling down. It's easy to think and feel, "We've made a lot of sacrifices to get this far. We deserve to settle down."

And it's not just pastors who think like this. I find business people everywhere with the same mentality. Starting a business is not easy; pioneering a work has challenges that most people know little to nothing about. You can't have a million-dollar dream with minimum-wage work ethic. The principle of making a million dollar dream come true is not that hard. In principle, all you have to do is provide value of a million dollars for other people. They'd be willing to pay you that million dollars with no problem. That's the simple principle of it. Anybody can do that. But you can't do it with an eight-to-five work mentality. It will take a very high level of dedication and some persistence over time to reach it. And so, we find business people everywhere who get to the point where their personal income gets to just a little above average. At that level, they can live at a certain level of personal comfort and many will often plateau there. To go from there to the next level, the level where you really start having some influence, takes a lot of effort. You've got to put forth the same kind of effort (or more) that you had to go through in order to start that business. And most people are not willing to do it because there is enough comfort to stay at the level they've already attained. Pastors do it. Business people do it. "Everybody" does it. But not us. That's not me. That's not us. That should not be people of faith. That mindset should be limited to people who are willing to settle for less than what God called them to do. Since you're still reading this, I don't believe you're willing to settle either! There is a lost, dying, and hurting world, and unless we take this to heart, they will remain lost, dying, and hurting. We must keep growing in order to reach more people.

In our personal lives and ministry, there have been several occasions where we had the option of staying at the current level or going further with God. This does not mean that every opportunity to expand is from God. The Apostle Paul had to stay put at times when the Spirit would not allow him to go on (*see* Acts 16). And growing with God isn't all about numerical growth. Sometimes He will lead us into new areas. In 2012, just a few months after South Sudan gained independence as the world's youngest country, an opportunity came for us to train a whole network of several hundred pastors there. We had the people who could help, but as we started to plan training in South Sudan, we sensed in our hearts that the time was not right. It didn't make any logical sense. There was peace in the country, a large number of leaders who had needs, and the outlook was good. Yet, we knew the best thing for us was to obey and stay put. Very soon, we would be thankful we didn't take the opportunity as the country once again plunged into civil war in December of 2013.

But this South Sudan story is the exception for us, not the norm. God continually has new assignments for us. Just like in the parable of the talents,[45] when you manage well what has already been given to you, more gets added onto your plates.

Stepping Out on the Missions Field

Back in 2006, we sold our house and belongings in Tulsa, Oklahoma, put a few things in storage, and moved to Kenya with our five-month-old daughter. Leaving the comforts of home and moving to a new land brings lots of uncertainties. There are so many areas you have to grow in, from handling the immigration laws of the new land, to understanding the culture and the people, to finding new ways of communicating and connecting with family and friends who are on the other side of the world. Just navigating a simple thing like paying a water bill can be quite an adventure when you have to get setup on foreign payment systems and figure out how to receive the bill when there is no email and it doesn't come through the postal system. Yet, in the midst of all those adjustments, we kept focusing on the assignment and the reason we were there. In a few short months after we arrived, we launched Safari Bible School in April of 2006.

45 Matt. 25:14–30

During our first year in Kisumu, we had virtually no support and had to learn how to believe God. It is easy to learn about faith and even talk faith when you have a job or some sort of income. It's a whole other thing when your life's on the line and you can't see any way out from a natural perspective. But the Hall of Faith is full of people who had to trust God and expect Him to come through when there was no natural possibility.

We'd hid a little extra money in accounts that would be hard to reach and decided to believe that God would take care of us like He had said. In the fall of 2006, there was no money, food was scarce, and we needed airfare to get to Norway. My mind was having a heyday, with a constant bombardment of thoughts like, *Look at you, you faith preacher! Soon, everyone will see that you are a failure. Imagine what it will be like when you will have to beg family members to rescue you from this place.* I was teaching the subject of faith in the Bible school, and even while teaching I would have to control the constant thoughts of failure and defeat. But, we kept declaring the truth and made sure we spent sufficient time with God and in his Word that we were still at peace in our hearts even if negative thoughts kept coming. And we never shared with anyone what our needs were because faith never puts pressure on people.

To make a long story short, someone in Australia, where we had never been, found out about our travel plans, and gave my wife and daughter free tickets from their airline points. Then he contacted another friend who donated his credit card points to pay the taxes on the free mileage tickets. My wife and daughter traveled on exactly the dates we had announced, while I remained in Kenya to continue the work.

From those early years, we have countless stories of God's provision, and it often came at the last minute when food, money, and water had just run out. Learning to trust God in these smaller things is critical. David learned by taking out the lion and the bear while he was doing a minor shepherding job and no one else was around to witness. Had he not done so, he would have never been in a position to take out Goliath later.

A couple of years later, we were again looking to expand the school into more areas. One day, we left a meeting with pastors in Lodwar, Kenya, flew to Nairobi, and drove from there to Garissa, which was a six-hour drive. About halfway, at Mwingi, a couple of police officers joined us for security because the rest of the road would go through a remote desert area with bandits and terrorists nearby. A short while after the police officers came along, we hit some potholes very hard and ended up with a flat tire. Evening was fast approaching, we were in an insecure and risky area, and had to change to the spare before we finally arrived in Garissa after dark.

The next morning I preached in Garissa. I'd spent the last money I had on fuel, the hotel, and dinner the night before. The Honda CRV we were driving had just a little fuel left and a flat tire that still needed to be repaired. There wasn't enough money to fill the car. And it was unthinkable to not fix the tire before returning back to Mwingi. After I preached my heart out for the people in Garissa, the pastor took up a second offering. For a moment, I sensed some relief, thinking there would be enough to get me back to Mwingi. Instead, the second offering was for the pastor's travel expenses, as he was traveling to Mombasa the following day. I only had about five dollars left, and the ATM withdrawal fee was two or three dollars. I opted to buy just a little fuel, not fix the tire, and head back to Mwingi on Sunday afternoon. I prayed, and then said, "There will be enough gas to get to Mwingi and there will be air in all four tires until I get there." I knew full well this was risky naturally speaking, because the road was very remote and certainly not a safe place to get stranded. And there was no money to hire security to come with me.

Driving the three hours through that remote desert area, my mind was talking loudly to me the whole way, mostly concerned about running out of fuel or having a flat tire that couldn't be replaced with a spare. Long before reaching Mwingi, the low fuel light was on. Once again, the battle of faith was on, and I kept meditating on the same scriptures that built my faith in the first place. With a mind in turmoil, I maintained peace in my heart and held on to what I'd said. I would reach Mwingi on the gas I had and there would be air in all tires. There were still more road left than there was fuel in the tank, but I kept driving and thanking God along the way.

I finally reached Pastor Titus Munuve's office in Mwingi just before sunset. School was starting the next day. I was glad to have arrived, although I was hungry, had no money, and needed to pay for my room at the guest house that night. I shared none of our needs with him, but after he heard of our story from Lodwar and Garissa, he said, "Let's go take care of that flat tire." I didn't know how we would pay, but we went. When we got to the car, not only was the spare tire flat, but I had a puncture in another tire coming back from Garissa, and one of the other tires was almost down to the rim. God had done exactly what I had said—there was enough gas to get to Mwingi, and there would be air in the tires until I reached there. I had checked and there was air in the tires when I parked the car. We rolled down to the tire shop, and as we arrived, Rev. Munuve said he would pay for the repairs of both tires.

After getting the tires repaired, Rev. Munuve took me to a friend of his I had not yet met, Reverend Paul Ngandi. Pastor Ngandi offered us dinner, and even polished my shoes at the door while we ate. When you are down to nothing, your mind is screaming at you, and wanting you to act like a beggar, it's a breath of fresh air just to have someone polish your shoes. After a wonderful dinner, Rev. Munuve brought me to the guest house. It was getting late, and I would be teaching school the next morning. I'd stayed at the guest house before, but they had new management who'd implemented a new policy that you had to pay before you got your room. Still not knowing my situation, Rev. Munuve said, "Please don't bother this man. He is a man of God, but he is very tired and needs his rest. Don't worry, he will pay." They gave me the key, I got some rest, and the next day money came for me to pay for that hotel.

Without any pressure put on people, I simply trusted God and He took care of my food, transportation, and a room through the generosity of other people. Many such stories have happened to me over the years.

We had explored opening schools in Lodwar and Garissa, which I shared with you briefly earlier, and while those locations did not work out at the time, we did not give up. We had results from the existing campuses, but still felt we needed to reach further into more remote areas, areas where many people did not want to travel. We continued exploring other areas and soon found an opportunity at Garsen, about 100 miles from the Kenya-Somali border. At the time, there had been a history of security incidents in the area. Al Qeada's sister organization, Al-Shabaab, operated nearby, so few were willing to travel to the area. It certainly would have been easier for us to just keep running the schools we already had going and not add more work in this challenging area.

But had we not gone there, we would have done like the Israelites did. After they crossed the Jordan and saw the miracle of the walls of Jericho falling, they kept conquering land, city by city and village by village. Though Jericho had been a big miracle, and though they had many answers to prayer along the way, most of the other areas were conquered by natural means—training and swinging the sword. It was the same way for us opening several of our school campuses. There wasn't always a big spectacular miracle, but we just believed this was the right place and had to go through the normal methods of meeting with people and pastors in the area. It was work.

But after Israel had conquered sufficient land for the people to be reasonably comfortable, they stopped expanding. And after a while Joshua told them, "How long will you put off going in to take possession of the land, which the Lord, the God of your fathers, has given you?"[46] It is so easy to start walking with God, whether in business or in ministry, and then along the way settle down and become content. But people who walk by faith always walk

46 Josh. 18:10

with God knowing there is always something more to be done. So, we opened the Garsen campus, even though it would have been easier and more comfortable to just stay with what we had going or choose more comfortable areas.

Soon, we were getting testimonies from the pastors who came to the school in Garsen. Several of them expressed surprise that we were willing to travel to such remote locations to train them. They told us, "If you can come this far, we can go further." So they started going out into very remote and unreached communities that have never had a church and started churches in those unreached areas. Stories and results like these are common. When you are willing to step out and go further, you become a leader, and many others will often follow.

Plateau or Keep Building?

Pioneering and building is hard work, but after a while, we had several Bible school campuses. The results were evident because reports from graduates kept rolling in. Churches were growing, children ministries were born, other Bible colleges were started, some went on to start flourishing businesses, and the list went on and on. There was an opportunity to change things from the hectic and sometimes chaotic pioneering phase to managing and fine tuning the operations on the schools that were running.

But, in prayer, my wife and I separately kept hearing "Nairobi" even though we had not yet talked to one another about what we were praying. As we continued praying, we realized that the time had come to start a work in Nairobi.

Going to Nairobi would require a new level of finances, moving the family again, learning cosmopolitan Kenyan culture, building a new team, and a host of other activities. From experience, most every time we expand into a new kind of endeavor, the challenges get bigger. Sometimes the hindrances are natural and growing in knowledge on our part is required to overcome. At other times, the challenges can be spiritual, and the battle is largely one of staying in faith.

In January 2017, it felt like we were in Job's shoes. We had moved to Nairobi as a family, but more than everything went wrong that month. By mid year, we were to host our first East Africa Faith Conference, and the Bible college was starting three months later. We had deadlines and all kinds of pressure. There was leadership turmoil in a ministry in Europe we were helping. Then, we were dealing with a moral failure amongst our own leadership team in Africa. In addition, one of our good friends in Kisumu lost both his wife and his baby during childbirth. Then one of my friends in Europe committed suicide, leaving behind his wife and four young children. On top of this, our office manager in the United States abruptly and unexpectedly quit, leaving us without a financial lifeline, since almost all our support was coming from the United States. To top it all off, our main speaker for the upcoming conference had to cancel.

But, we were sure we were in the will of God. I learned long ago to never look at circumstances to determine if we were doing what God wanted us to do. Brother Hagin, the founder of Rhema Bible Training College where I attended, used to say, "I have passed up some marvelous opportunities to worry." We also had to pass through this season, putting our trust in God. I often thought of all of Paul's struggles and how he in the midst of it declared:

> **For we were so utterly burdened beyond our strength that we despaired of life itself ... But that was to make us rely not on ourselves but on God ... On him we have set our hope [expectant confidence] that he will deliver us again.**
>
> **2 Corinthians 1:8–10**

Before he was king, David was in a similar scenario. When he was chased by King Saul and rejected by King Achish, he came home to Ziklag with his team to discover that the Amalekites had burned down their city and captured their wives, children, and livestock. His own team became so distraught and bitter they wanted to kill David.

But David encouraged himself in the Lord his God.

1 Samuel 30:6 (KJV)

Just a short time later David became king.

As we were approaching the conference in May of 2017, we were dealing with many challenges, we put in long and hard days, and we still didn't have the funding. But regardless of circumstances, and though the thoughts might be hard to control, true faith in God will always have a peace and a joy in your heart. One late evening, we headed to bed. I was exhausted, my muscles were aching, and I was about to drift to sleep around midnight. My mind was still on the funding for the conference. I caught myself meditating on doubt and unbelief and realized I must not go to sleep in such a condition. Yet, my mind seemed to be shouting, "You have had enough today! Just go to sleep! You need the rest!" Instead of letting my mind and feelings control me, I got up in the middle of the night, went to our small living room, and started going over the promises of God, His faithfulness, and meditating on scriptures. It took a while to conquer the doubt, but after a while, the joy and peace of true faith returned. I kept meditating and praising, and around two o'clock that morning, I was literally dancing before God in our living room. A few days later, the money came and at four o'clock on Tuesday afternoon, we could finally cut the check for the venue. The business office closed an hour later, which was our deadline for payment. But the conference started the next morning, just as we had believed.

We could have been comfortable with a few campuses in Kenya. People were celebrating the results, and there were many testimonies. But we also knew there is always more when we walk with God. We thank God for the comforts of a good house, a good car, and so forth. We believe in those things and we have those things. But those are not the top of the list.

> **But seek first the kingdom of God and his righteousness, and all these things will be added to you.**
>
> **Matthew 6:33**

But we primarily seek something more besides our own needs being met. We seek for our own lives to be poured out for the benefit of other people. We seek to live our lives in such a way that others will be impacted for the sake of the kingdom of God. Such is a life that is lived by faith in God and using our faith for assignments.

CHAPTER FIVE

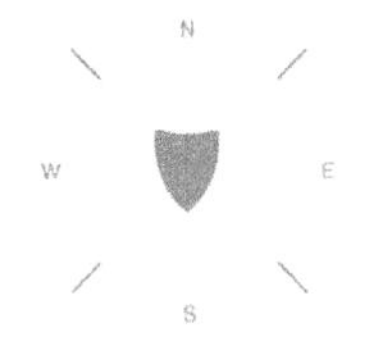

No Shrinking Back

Therefore do not throw away your confidence, which has a great reward. For you have need of endurance, so that when you have done the will of God you may receive what is promised. For, "Yet a little while, and the coming one will come and will not delay; but my righteous one shall live by faith, and if he shrinks back, my soul has no pleasure in him." But we are not of those who shrink back and are destroyed, but of those who have faith and preserve their souls.

Hebrews 10:35–39

Faith Does Not Shrink Back

Shrinking back is not okay. Not living by faith is not okay. Just because we had one successful season of life doesn't mean it's time to sit down and relax. Faith never relaxes. People of faith are those who take the kingdom of God by force. After Peter got out of the boat, and quit believing, Jesus rebuked him. Jesus rebuked the disciples for not being able to heal the father's son, who came to him while Jesus was on the Mount of Transfiguration. Most preachers today would put the problem on the father and say, "There's a problem with your faith." The problem was not with the faith of the father; the problem was with the faith of the disciples.

Know your God, be a person of action, live by faith, and do more than what you could do in your own natural strength.

It is not okay to not have faith. It's not okay to not use our faith. It is not okay to not progress. It's not okay to not influence society. It's not okay to not pursue the dream God has given us. Faith is the only way to please God. He expects us to walk by it.

A Final Appeal

What is the next level for you as an individual? What is the next stage for us as a church, business, or whatever assignment God has given us.

Therefore since we are surrounded by such a great cloud of witnesses, let us lay aside every

weight and sin which clings so closely. And let us run with endurance the race that is set before us.

Hebrews 12:1–2

Where will you go from here? What is your next assignment? For some, it will be like Paul after he finished his ministry in Asia; he reached new territories continuing the same ministry but reaching further.

For others, it will be like David. He went from herding sheep to making music for the king. Your transition could be similar where you find yourself doing something completely new.

Others may need to do like Solomon, take the foundation someone else built and continue it into a new level of prosperity.

For yet others, they might be like Phillip, where they are given a special assignment in order to reach one person like Phillip and the Eunuch of Ethiopia.

Or maybe the next assignment is like Stephen and Phillip earlier in their life, simply engaging in the needs of the local church and becoming faithful deacons.

Whichever it is, do like they all did in the Hall of Faith. Know your God, be a person of action, live by faith, and do more than what you could do in your own natural strength.

We are waiting for His soon return. Let us be like those the prophet Daniel spoke of, saying in the midst of turmoil and difficult times:

> **but the people that do know their God shall be strong, and do exploits.**
>
> **Daniel 11:32 (KJV)**

Benediction

As this book concludes, I hope you have found a new passion, determination, and level of faith to go after the next assignment God has placed on your life. It won't always be easy, but it will be worth it!

As your next act of faith, pray the following prayer as you prepare for your next assignment:

Father, thank You for Your Word. I commit and dedicate myself to go where You want me to go, to say what You want me to say, and to do what You want me to do. Give me wisdom and insight into Your will and Your plan. I commit to be faithful to steward what You give me to do. Thank you, Father! I pray all of this in Jesus' name. Amen.

ABOUT THE AUTHOR

Since 1999, Vidar Ligard has been a catalyst for change in East Africa, dedicating his life to nurturing leadership and personal growth. His practical, Bible-based teachings have empowered countless individuals to emerge as influential leaders, fostering community development and inspiring action.

Through his work with Bible schools and seminars, Vidar has been instrumental in guiding people to overcome poverty, expand churches, establish successful enterprises, combat corruption, and mold leaders who positively affect thousands daily.

Alongside his wife, Cathrine, Vidar founded Safari Mission, an organization committed to social and spiritual advancement. He is based in Nairobi, where he and Cathrine raise their four daughters and continue to contribute to the flourishing of their community.

FINDING JESUS

Faith for assignments is great, but it doesn't matter if you don't put your faith in Jesus first. He died on the cross for you, your sins, and so you can have peace with God. If you have never asked Jesus to be your Lord and Savior or maybe you need to rededicate your life to Him, simply pray the following prayer:

> *Dear God, I come to You right now in the name of Jesus. I know that I am a sinner, and I confess my sins to You. I confess with my mouth that Jesus is Lord, and I believe in my heart that You raised Him from the dead. Because of that, I thank You that I am saved, and I have peace with You. In Jesus name I pray,*
>
> *Amen.*

If you prayed this prayer, I would love to hear from you. You can reach me at office@safarimission.org

SAFARI
MISSION
Training Leaders and Transforming People in East Africa.

Listen to edifying and lifechanging teachings from Revs. Vidar and Cathrine Ligard, Founders and Directors of Safari Mission and Rhema Kenya.

The podcasts are free to listen to and you can find them on various platforms like YouTube, Facebook, Apple Podcast, Spotify, Buzzsprout, etc.

Scan the QR code to find us easily.